MY SISTERS' COUNTRY

Kore Press, Inc

A Division of Kore Press Institute
325 West Second Street, #201
Tucson, AZ 85705
www.korepress.org

Sisters by Gwendolyn Brooks, *Reprinted By Consent of Brooks Permissions.*
Cover Art: "Antithesis" © copyright Dawn Okoro
Design by Sally Geier

We express gratitude to the National Endowment for the Arts, the Arizona
Commission on the Arts through appropriations for the Arizona State Legislature,
the Literary Arts Emergency Fund, the Arts Foundation for Tucson and Southern
Arizona, and to individuals for support to make this Kore Press Institute
publication possible.

ISBN 978-1-888553-79-6

Library of Congress Cataloging-in-Publication
DataNames: Jackson, Alexis V., 1990- author. Title: My sisters' country / Alexis V.
Jackson. Description: Tucson : Kore Press, 2022. Identifiers: LCCN 2021036185 |
ISBN 9781888553796 (trade paperback) Subjects: LCGFT: Poetry. Classification:
LCC PS3610.A3448 M8 2021 | DDC 811/.6--dc23 LC record available at https://
lccn.loc.gov/2021036185

WORDS
OF
BLACK
WOMEN
&
BLACK
GIRLS
IN
OUTLINE

JUST AS
WORDS
OF
CHRIST ARE
IN RED
IN MANY
VERSIONS
OF THE
GOSPELS

Table of Contents

Sisters,
where there is cold silence
no hallelujahs, no hurrahs at all, no handshakes,
no neon red or blue, no smiling faces
prevail.
Prevail across the editors of the world
who are obsessed, self-honeying and self-crowned
in the seduced arena.

It has been a
hard trudge, with fainting, bandaging and death.
There have been startling confrontations.
There have been tramplings. Tramplings
of monarchs and of other men.

But there remain large countries in your eyes.
Shrewd sun.

The civil balance.
The listening secrets.
And you create and train your flowers still.

Gwendolyn Brooks
To Black Women

Dear Mom,

You wanted me when God didn't. Told me to love Him anyway. Told me you had no business actin' simple with that [self-censoring pause] man, but I was a blessing. "A Blessing mommy?" "A blessing, little girl." "Your blessing?" "My blessing." And all of this just was. Like it was wanting to be something else, but it couldn't because ~~y~~You said it. But somewhere tween leaving ~~y~~Your house and askin' God about Him and him and HIM and him & him, ~~y~~You wanted me and ~~God~~ He didn't. And I didn't know how to recon that with my still being. Didn't know if that made you You or God or GOD or god or HER or her. Maybe I wouldn't be so close to textbook anxious if you'd done what ~~He~~ God said. Maybe I wouldn't be so sad about the word "depravity" and about sinsickness existing and about people pushing past kids for trains if ~~yY~~you'd done what God said. If you'd done what God said, maybe you'd be happier maybe you'd be more like Christ and less like all the heathens heathening without thinkin bout not heathening. Mommy, how do ~~y~~You look at ~~y~~Your sin and love her? How do ~~y~~You teach her to be Her and still need Him who made you cry cuz of ~~h~~Her, made You stop working with the church children cuz of Her, made You think You not worthy cuz of Her? I really want Your answer cuz you Him and him and her and Her to me. And I need to know who to be someday so if I want someone God doesn't, I can know how to answer like ~~Y y Y y Y y Y you Adrienne Anna~~ "My blessing" "My blessing" "My blessing" "My blessing" "My blessing" "My blessing," and know it.

Hos And Grandmas And Aunties Be Like

They want the pussy, but they don't want the people
They want the pussy, but they don't want the problems
They want the pussy, but they don't want the person
They want the pussy, but they don't want the

                                        person

They want the pussy, but they don't want the person?
They want the pussy,

                    but they don't want the people

They want the pussy, but they don't want

                                the people

They want the pussy, but

                    they don't want

                        the people

         the PUSSY

They want   , but they don't want

                          the people

They want the pussy, but they don't want the problem
They want the pussy, but they don't want the problem
They want the pussy,

                    but you, Sweetness,...

They want the pussy, but they don't want the person
They want the pussy, but they don't want no whole of this
They want the pussy, but they don't want the whole

They want the pussy, but they don't want the sparkle

                   but they don't want the spirit

                   but they don't want the stuff

                   but they don't want the scent

They want the pussy,

                   but you, Glory...

                     they don't want the problem

                     they don't want the problems

                     they don't want the people

                     they don't want the sparkle

They want the pussy, but
They want the pussy, but
They want the pussy, but   they don't want
                     they don't want
                     they don't want
                     they don't want,

                                   but you

When We Prayed

When we prayed for
4 little Black girls—
brains, bodies and bows
blown at Baptist Siloam
by terrorist with easy name
and all American face—
after ejaculated bombs
left blood-stained satin
in rubble of sanctified
red brick, once holy of holies,

what
were they
wearing?

Don't worry love.

That Spirit Day
in your Christian academy
when the teacher pointed
out you and your friends'
cut up uniform shirts

that last Spirit Day
when y'all were rockin' em
over white tees and beaters
to let em know y'all wasn't
never coming back

that day when
the teacher doubled over
through laughing tears
croaked up "You girls
look like prostitutes"

you were barely 18
and not quite in
the best position
to bore into her blue eyes
and break her god

Oh, but daughter
fret not
for such
a time
as this

Blue-Brown

For Renisha McBride, Korryn Gaines, Diamond and Dae'Anna Reynolds,...

My niece runs her hand across
the top of my car.
She calls it maybe black—
says it might be navy—
but she can't tell in the dark.

She is 7.
She grabs her tilted afro puff
and asks me what color it is. I say brown.
She says I'm right, but
some of the kids in her class
think it's black.
She says she tells them
it's brown.
She says her ballies are blue—
true blue, she says—the blue
you can see at night time.

She snakes her fingers through mine.
At the crosswalk she says the street
is black.
She says the outsides of my "throw on slides" are blue—
a blue different from her sister's track bag—
the blue that looks like someone's favorite color.
She tells me that's her favorite color.
She asks me for mine.
I tell her black.

She calls us Black.
She says we're not black like my car,
or the street, or my favorite color, or
the mesh on the sides of her sister's track bag
that lets the stuff inside breathe.
We're the Black that's really brown, like
her mommy says her puff is, like
the floor in her new house is, like

my eyes, not
maybe brown—like
some cars are really navy—but in the dark
and in the day
everybody else
can't tell sometimes.

We use our free hands
to make shadow puppets jump
in the porch light
until my brother
answers the door
and she lets go.

Crooked Room

When I finally touch you
I won't ever remember holding
My breath

These lengths of time
Like 1 Mis·sis·sip·pi
2 Mis·sis·sip·pi
3 Mis·sis·sip·pi
4 M-I-
Crooked Letter Crooked Letter I
Trace crooked letters down the lining of your jaw

Blue in the face
River clay
Your ear ends taste like salt and vinegar
And that's just fine

I still call you candy
King and Angel and Baby Love

We still talk about Fish River Canyon
Like Namibia is up the street gettin' redone
Like they'll let us in after the reno

And about the ice cream canyon crater
In my butter pecan
That we can't remember whose spoon
Carved Playing spoons
And the dozens with our legs laced together
"Yo mama so ugly
Rice Krispies won't talk to her"
"Yo mama so dumb
She went to the dentist for a Bluetooth"
Whose mama gave who what crooked
Big and second shovel-lookin' toe

Shit!

I burned the bacon
And you haven't touched my eggs

And Gwendolyn Brooks wrote something about burnt breakfast
And bleak *ballads* of *Dark Villain[s]* and *milk-white maid[s]*

And you're already thinking of *The Negro Speaks of Rivers*
And being born by the river
And I'm thinking of Vine's viral version
Rih, Rih, Rih, I was born by the river. I was shakin' dat ass

And it's been too hard living
With nothing but the idea of you

I write these crooked poems
With the idea of you
When I'm worried about
Them having the wrong idea of you
So you'll never come home

And from the crooked system's cell
You'll write crooked letters
Crooked letter I

Find all transit lines lead to the end of the road
And everything can lead to 90s R&B
Or a musical score trapped
In the yellow brick
Trapped in the yellow wall paper

Yellow or red-boned is something I am not
Cooked marrow is closer to the true
Color of my skin
So you don't put me in songs
Or club sonnets

And
That's just
Fine cuz I do

And I'm just fine
Until you reach for my waist
And I'm wonderin'
Why you want
What doesn't
Make you sing
Why you want

Lady in brown
dark phrases of womanhood

o o o

Half notes scattered

Crooked down
Across

Crooked room

Cdnt figure out whose hand was on my thigh/

But it didn't matter

I must have wanted it

I was the one who missed the train

Who made the dinner

Who wore the red silk

And the whole smile

And the waxed brows

And the Nile and the Tigris and the Euphrates

And Malaysian curly
And the catfish and cheese grits thickness

[And] dark red ribbons in my hair
milk tea on your fingers
the wood burns white all night
you pull in and out of me
until I'm plump with love
round enough to eat

If I wasn't so damn Fertile
Crescent like

I'd be able to stop growing
To stop growing them
To stop producing cash crop kids—more arid, good land
To stop looking like good land
Like Canaan like second Eden
Like the well and the drain
Delta stewardess said
To count while my gum pops
To make this part easy

I think of her
With you here
And I start

Inhale

Counting

Hunchback
Hunchback

I
Saw a snake
In my Bible
Between the beginnings
How strange to see it on legs
With arms and feet
Handing mother a clementine
Cuz it was jealous

And just mean

I think I saw it in the pledge of allegiance
And in the tent meeting
And strung between your hands
When you laid em on Lillie Blue
And told her she'd be forgiven
For dancing with Eddie Sherman

When all she was doin'
Was dancin'
With someone
Who wants
To love her

My Sisters' Country

In the moments after his mania,
I pick eggshell shrapnel out of my sisters' eyes
and ears
and memories
in my grandmother's kitchen.

We hard-boil hearts and devil them—
room temperature bite-size servings
that put the meat back on our bellies,
that keep us possible.

We crack open the calabash and cleanse
with proverbs and the fantastic about the
women before the women before the
women before us who homed with the
men before the men before the men before
him.

My mother
compares her recipes to the myths'.
My grandmother ices our feet.
My sisters
count their scars.
I
watch.

My mother leads them back
to our home,
to their rooms,
to him,
to a fresh dozen.

I follow.

I am wondering why we leave my
grandmother's kitchen,

Why we leave holding each other
to hold cold yolk and white,

to sweep up the aborted chicken fetus
cocoon pieces,

for atomic warhead him.
Why I leave watching for warring.

We hear our mother try
a different way of whisking.

We hear him
plead
Blackamericanmanhypermasculitiyenza
for war crimes.

My mother forgives without promise
of reparations.

My sisters build a country in me.

I build a country in my grandmother's
kitchen.

Here, the women have calloused feet
and nimble fingers. Here, it is criminal
for men to make breakfast. Here,
Mars wears red nail polish
and the scent of *White Diamonds,* and
and I watch her
watch me
spoil.

The Man And The Me On The Bus

He sits
I offer the outlet next to me because
The girl who was here before me
made me nervous to ask her
He says thank you
And asks if I am writing a poem
I wish I wasn't writing a poem
I say I'm writing a poem
And he tells me he writes acrostics
Only he can't remember the word acrostic
He tells me he does them with names
And somehow I know they're bad
And he tells me I have beautiful sweet lips
And I wish I hadn't worn lipstick
And I remember the woman at the museum
Who was staring at me instead
Who told me I was beautiful
And I think I have anxiety
Except I don't
Because the doctor said I failed the test
And the acrostic wouldn't work because
He doesn't know me
And what do you do when you get to the X?
He seemed nice, but so did I
And that's no fault of mine But I feel like it is
And how would I tell him to leave
When he has to be next to me
In the rain
With the angry bus driver
Who's driven 400,000 miles without an accident
And the woman who wanted him to fix the beeping noise
And the broken bus
We all transferred from
That made us late
Maybe I should've stayed
Or shouldn't have come
Or shouldn't have wanted to go

Someone yells *kick her off the bus*
The poem is finished
And he's sleeping
Until he's not
And wants to know
If he can walk me to my ride
And I'll cry later
Because I'll remember how scared I was
How long I didn't blink
When I say no
Without saying no
And he moves his knee
And asks me to say I love you
In Spanish
On the Greyhound
I can't fall asleep
The rain sounds like the slowed down version
Of me twisting open my ginger ale
And the amplified Velcro
of lashes separating
blinking
In heavy rotation

Therapy Session Number 1

My weakness is sunbreak and indigo crayons and that purple pen cap behind the couch next to the penny I keep heads up—part curated luck, part seat-sniffing crack. What are knots anyway? Aren't there smaller questions you ask yourself on the train that make you a lie your mother forgets she tells, a lie the vending machine and turnstile need? Then there's the red seaweed and our entire, polyester-clad bodies and my hair expanding then shrinking like us meeting and professing then becoming actual. I think the rain in Jerusalem smells like it should, but what do I care. Of what consequence is any "singular" "this" if my grandmother reads all about us, and says I skipped too many spots, missed too many canon mundanities, for her to call it true—for it to be just right enough

for good?

When The Water Comes

When the water comes—
not when it rains
or when it spills, sugared, from a pitcher
or boils over, salted, from pot or kettle
but when it really comes—
Will I dis solve
Will there be enough flesh to make a salve paste
Will it taste
Will it libate
Will I float—wombed vessel, ark, two
of every kind of evil and good and myth
and magic and numbers and fabrics and talents
and songs and grips and blesses and curses and dream
dream

Will I sink—
standing incanting
filling imbibed
swelling like Buckwheat's mammy mother's voice
in black girls' hands playing house with a head rag
perm swaddled and gait waddled
fighting instead of flighting
needing goggled eyes
to see without sting when opening

lying on my belly to keep my strands from shrinking
Will I dig a hole in the water
for my unborn and for their milk—
let my back char
get consumed
tilt my head to bubble bubble breathe breath
bubble
bubble
breathe breath
bubble
bubble
breathe breath

Will I know that it's water and not death
not skeet
not squirt
not piss
not cream soda
not blood
not vinegar
not wine
not
mine

Kind of god,
Will you remember how to use it—
speak wade away your scent in wait for low chariot
Will you have to
Will it cleanse—
disinfect
stop
cool white smell of burning brown scalp, leaving
pink scabbing flesh

Will it need a chaser—
conditioning oil or ointment
running over
running over
dripping dribbling over everything that saw its reflection
before being consumed
baptized dunked dropped
daft dapped damned damp dank thing

When the water comes—
not misting during a midday jog
or filling a stopped up toilet
but when it really comes

Will the aftermath
be after

or did I miss it

or are we always drowning

or am I water
coming

or am I water
always
almost
about to
come

I Went Inside Myself

Found
A hymn hum moan
A shout for salvation
A prayer for food
And the head of a prophet
screaming

Blues Club Dance Music Mashup
(feat. Bessie Smith, Nina Simone, Eartha Kitt, Viola Davis, & Beyoncé)

Why don't you love me

        Why you wanna fly blackbird

Why don't you love me

        Why you wanna fly blackbird

Why don't you love me

        Why you wanna fly

Why don't you love me

        Why you wanna fly blackbird

Why don't you love me

        Why you wanna fly blackbird

Why don't you love me

        Why you wanna fly

Why you wanna fly
Why you wanna fly
Why you wanna fly
Why you wanna

Why don't you   *wanna fly blackbird*
Why don't you   *love me*

Why don't you   *wanna fly blackbird*
Why don't you   *love me*

Why don't you   *wanna fly blackbird*
Why don't you   *love me*
When I make me so damn easy

        You ain't never gonna   *love me*
        You ain't never gonna   *love me*
        You ain't never gonna   *love me*

Tell me baby why don't you

COMPROMISE!

When you fall in love, what is there to compromise about?

The gods have been very good to me, and the people, My fans have been absolutely wonderful to me. And they're the ones who adopted me. They're the ones who made me feel worthwhile. But no one person ever did that. And I'm not talkin' about my daughter Kitt, that's an adage in itself, but no one person has ever come into my life and made me feel so great as the audience has. That's why I say, every time I'm on that stage, I'm always afraid I'm going to be given away. So I'm constantly, with my soul, actually begging.

COMPROMISE!

                              love me

actually begging
COMPROMISE!

                              love me

actually begging
COMPROMISE!

                              love me

actually begging
COMPROMISE!

                    love me

                         so damn easy
                         so damn easy
                         so damn easy
                         so damn easy
                         so damn easy
                         so damn easy
                         so damn easy to

                              Never   LLL Love me
                                        Love me

LLL Love me
Love me
LLL Love me
Love me
LLL Love me
Love me
LLL Love me

Tired of being blue

blackbird

Tired of being blue   *blackbird*

Tired of being blue

blackbird

Tired of being blue   *blackbird*

Tired of being blue

I fall in love with myself and I want someone to share it with me

share it

with me

share it

with me

share it

with me

share it

with me

me me me

me me me

me me me

eee eee

eee ee eee

eee eee

e e e e e e e e

e e e e e

Check my credentials!

Why don't you love me

with   my   soul,

Why don't you love me

actually begging with

Why don't you love me

my   soul,   actually

Why don't you love me

begging *Why you wanna*

Why don't you love me

fly

Why don't you love me

W h y   y o u
w a n n a   fly
actually begging

I'm always afraid

You ain't never gonna   *love me*
You ain't never gonna   *love me*
You ain't never gonna   *love me*
You ain't never gonna

Check my credentials!

When you have, I don't know, say me coming in as someone's love interest. It doesn't compute because no one thinks I'm pretty. No one thinks a Black woman who's darker than a paper bag is pretty. They don't think she's sexual. They find her more mannish. They associate her probably more with a man, more earthy, more soulful, more sassy. You know, I see you more with an apron than I do see you naked rolling around in bed with someone. Because that is

so damn easy
so damn easy
so damn easy
so damn easy
so damn easy
so damn easy
so damn easy
so damn easy

Don't play Yourself!

17 Black Church Girl Blues

1. We are crusaders
2. We are soldiers
3. A little bit louder
4. More more more
5. In the army (of the Lord)
6. We have to fight although we have to die
7. Examine the "we"
8. You cannot be a "we"
9. [I] have to hold up the blood-stained banner
10. I can be a you: U
11. I, you, me have to hold it up until one of we dies
12. Behold the fowls. Be like them—trusting, unworried and righteous.
13. Niggas always quick to call a bitch a bird
14. I don't have feathers nigga
15. Just like I don't have hazel eyes or a fat ass, but you knew that
16. We know that

50 Feet of Plastic

wrapped around your daughters'
hands. I was made for her, her friends,
you. Hear me clack clap the tar, watch
her jump back—pull out her arm fast
when I whoosh then crack snap
against her soft. She'll tie me
around her arms, bundle me into a braid.
I'll be the O shape hanging
on her neck while she skips,
sometimes drags, herself home.

Jump Rope

BoomBoom Tang Tang
Fitting footsies between the whites
Of clotheslines
Holding the half-grown glands
And the hoops down down baby
Barefoot
BoomBoom Tang Tang
Out to ends
Never beating the second Tang
Never passing footsies.
The shame of a baby doll turn
Isn't worth it.
BoomBoom Tang Tang
Tight rope skipping
Ain't easy.
Catching waterfalls
Cuz its hot, and you used
Your dollar on ice cream.
BoomBoom Tang
Remembering what part
She got out on. Pushing the air in the
Middle rhythm of the rope before the jump
In. Turning non-flicted to keep from hearing
Something in the rope ain't right.
Lemme get a jump real quick
from any whom means
Sharing if she shared last week or yesterday. And you gotta
BoomBoom
Loop ya rope just right to keep from knots. The
braid or the gimp or the giant circle around
Your elbows.
But everyday y'all at it.
BoomBoom Tang Tang
BoomBoom Tang Tang
BoomBoom Tang Tang

Then a man in a car

Then his
Can I get a turn?

And we shatter

Fresh Princess Sonnets

I.

We were pigtailed, beaded, ballied porch gods.
5-8 an' Catharine on West Philly's edge.
We ont play wit nobody off our block.
We ont tawk to no mayun callin' ova no headge.
We got dat R-E-E-B-O-K hop.
Roun' here we ont play no London bridge.
That stuff's for babies, and babies we not.
We get corner store *Hugs* and mommy's bread
and *Homegirl Chips* all by ourself. Eat hot
sunflower seeds, make real Spice Girl bets
like, "betchu I could be a betta Posh."
Scept no one be Scary Spice in pretend.
Had to be her enough when we not here.
Had to be her all the time when we not.

II.

Had to be her all the time, but the thing is, Aunt Viv was from Philly too,
lyyyke dark skin aunt Viv killed that dance scene *for* Philly, lyyyke
dark skin aunt Viv was a professor *for* Philly. Like, dark skin Aunt Viv was
dark skin Philly girls winning— dark skin, skinny, Philly girls winning yo.
Taking care of they *damn* nephews who get in trouble in they
neighborhood cuz that's just what we do. She was a whole
fuckin' doctor yo. Lyyyyke she was a bomb professor, a bomb wife, a
bomb mom. Yo, what couldn't she do, bruh?
My nigga, she had a whole notha baby, wit whole grown ass kids, and
was happy. I never heard nobody's brother or daddy say she was Claire
Huxtable fine tho.I never heard nobody saying they wanted to look like
her or be a professor like her tho.
But, feel me on this yo, dark skin Aunt Viv was from Philly, wit her *own*
shit, and was happy.

III.

Our own shit—Happy Black History month pageants on Larchwood Ave.
in Philadelphia Christian Academy's lunchroom/auditorium/music room.
Recitations: [Waving hot combs] *My name is Madame C.J Walker*
[Waving papers] *My name is Langston Hughes*

I Too Sing America
I Too Sing America
[Waving Bible] *My name is Dr. Martin Luther King Jr.*
[Waving microphone] *My name is Oprah Winfrey*
Does my sassiness offend you?
And *"lonely the road we trod"*
And *"We've come this far by faith"*
And lil' Black children swimming in they parent's clothes
buying dollar office hot plate hot dogs for lunch; *full of the*
hope that the present has brought us; facing the rising sun

IV.

I went to private school in the suburbs,
the other kids thought I lived in the "hood."
When they saw my row home near the airport, they said "We didn't know you
had like a real house." The teacher's said "She is so polite, and so bright."
We had "chapel service," and I didn't know it was church because we didn't
church like this. So I studied in the auditorium while they contemporary
christianed, and a teacher asked me if I struggled with joy. She was white. All
the teachers, except the one who told us not to be hoochie mamas, were white.
But they had a real kitchen and a real auditorium and real speakers in
classrooms. And enough Black girls to make a clique. And Jesus. And money.
And college-prep on the website—where it looked like more Black people were
there than true. When I finally made it on the website, I didn't know how to feel.
My grandmother, and my aunt, and my dad, and my mom paid my tuition,
and showed everyone.

V.

Don't show nobody your hair *Bald-headed skidddle diddle*
Pam, Dijonay, Kelly,
Roach
African Booty Scratcher
Must be ya ass cuz it ain't ya face
Ain't got no hair in the middle
You can't be Beyoncé
Girl where your weave at? You know you need that.
You so dark your blood type burnt.
How you have African roots and Indian hair?
Want a *Yellow model chick*
Should be *Lookin' Trinidadian, Japanese and Indian*

Witcho chocolate ass,
You can't be Penny Proud, ha, you can be Oscar though.

VI.

[She tell me] meet her in the bathroom
so she can tell me about her first time in secret,
show me the passion marks,
pray.
White girls gone wild, we ont judge em tho they ain't on trial
They're our prayer partners. They're in our accountability circles.
Pray. Say she want to try a Black guy cuz she heard it's bigger. Tell you when
you're married, it'll really hurt cuz of course he'll be big and Black and ready cuz
he used to *fuck bitches by the group.* Now he has to be full with just you.
Pray for purity and the power to be enough.
She think everybody want you cuz she wants your lips, and your eyes, and your
ass. She don't know they all sing to her—gimme that Becky and make me
white as snow. She asks for your prayer request, for what you're trusting God for.
Then tries to touch your hair.

VII.

My hair is in its natural state sometimes and Pennsylvania and New York
see it and do nothing. My body is in its unnatural state most of the time
like in this poem. I see it and think it belongs nowhere culture isn't.
Is this poem for the cul·ture? What I am teaching is a class on knives and
cheesesteaks and how to build a home on the tip of the dick your woman relocated
you to. How to make friends there with the dick's deities and learn the dick's
lang·u·age. How to keep yourself holy while making life around the habits of the
dick. I think this class is on how all white people don't, but all white people have,
and all white people are all white people, and I'm one of a few things to them,
but I can only be what I think you think I am so what came first—the black
woman or what what what what then?
My favorite word is me and my favorite place is always Boathouse Row and
my mother. Fuck subject verb agreement, and let me pretend Nu'Bia's just...
a'ight.

Some Words Bedevil, **But My Self-Care Playlist Lit Tho**

1. Said lil' bitch, you can't fuck with me if you wanted to. See it's two types of bitches in the world. That's right, and then you got a bitch like me. That bitch.

2. I am God's greatest hit. Considered above the angels, a fearfully made bitch.

3. My shit. Big lips and big big big hips. Body be thick like a biscuit. Dis [all] my shit.
   [Let me tell you how I got it]: rule number 1 to be a boss ass bitch, never let a clown nigga try to play you.

   > a) You bitches better have my money, or I'm coming for you. Cuz I'm a boss ass bitch bitch bitch bitch

4. It is better to speak/remembering/ we were never meant to survive [this].

5. bitch bitch bitch. Shit I'm the baddest. The baddest, baddest. My pussy's the phattest I'm representin' for these bitches. All eyes on your riches. Got an ass like the sun. But I'm finna make it rain on you bitches.

6. I am God's greatest hit. Considered above the angels, a fearfully made bitch.

7. Any happiness you get you've got to make yourself. Make 'em witness.

8. That's what boss bitches do. Order rich bitch sauce. Queen bitch. Supreme bitch. I'm rich. Ima stay dat bitch. I'ts my shit. I'm THAT BITCH. Bow down bitch/ Bow down bitch/Bow down bitchessssss/ H Town bishesssssssss.

9. RESISTANCE. RESISTANCE.

10. I'm so crown/ Bow down bitchessssssssss/ Still can't stand them bitchessssssss/ Because I'm rich, y'all/ and I'm a bitch, y'all/ A rich bitch y'all/ A rich bitch y'all

11. Any happiness you get you've got to make yourself. Make 'em witness.

12. RESIST SIS.

13. That's right, and then you got a bitch like/[I]. The capital B means I'm bout that life/ The capital B means I'm bout that life.

14. Didn't drop from the moon just last midnight.

15. I heard your boo was talkin' lip.

16. I told my crew to smack that trick. Smack that trick. Smack that trick. Guess what they did, smack that trick. Now I'm all the way up. So, bitch shut the fuck all the way up.

17. I am God's greatest hit. Considered above the angels, a fearfully made bitch.

18. Pay me what you owe me. Bitch better have my money.
19. I'm That Bitch—bitch—bitch—bitch—bitch—bitch—bitch
20. That's right.
21. I'm a boss ass bitch. Ouchea, speakin', survivin' and shit.
    a. it is better to speak/remembering/we were never meant to survive [this shit].
22. So when y'all see me in the street./ This is what I want y'all to do./ Fix your lips, put 'em together nicely and say/ Say it along, say it along now, say/ SHE'S A BITCH!

Themed Zuihitsu: My Fourth Great Grandmother and God and Me

Sitting in church
Shut out
Shut down

Closed eyes and bowed head
My skeletal X-ray looking close to broken

I've prayed so oft
That eyelids have grown callous
And neck has trouble remembering the strength to hold up
And knees have turned red from sanctuary carpet dye
And tongues sound like sensical sentences that don't
daunt the devil into dictionary he can't understand
And palms have crossfit coursed holding palms and floors
And altars and oil and waiting and
Jacob's ladder

And This
This
This
This indefinite amening in Black Jesus' name
Is not enough to stop violence in Syria, violence in Flint's pipes,
Violence in US justice systems, Killing, Killing, Killing
Kneeling posture
In sanctuary
Next to sanctuers
Doesn't stop the world from breaking
And I am afraid that I am beginning
To learn silence in the presence of the Lord
And absence in the presence of the truth

I am afraid that the killing is killing my God
Taking that from me too
Means they've won, erasure,
And I'm left wondering whose image I came from
Looking so unlike them
Looking so unlike them

Looking so unlike them
Looking so unlike them
Looking so unlike them
Looking so unlike them

Benediction

Lined up against the playground fence
Waiting to be picked
Wanting to be picked first

Rosa Etta picked me
Taught me how to play miss Mary Mack
In the right bottom of America
Taught me how to find and hide in the creases
Between Alabama and Georgia and the Carolinas and
Virginia until dropping me North

I [...]remember silent walks in
Southern woods and long talks
In low voices
Shielding meaning from the big ears
Of overcurious adults.

I remember
Skipping rope
Skipping stones
Stuffing brown dolls for pretend
Playing like brown girls survive on purpose
As omniscient gods who set things up like this to show
Our immortality

be-
cause [we] have been wrong the wrong sex the wrong age
the wrong skin the wrong nose the wrong hair the
wrong need the wrong dream the wrong
geographic the wrong sartorial

You ever read the passage about God opening up the ground and swallowing
up all the disobedient and wonder why God don't swallow up all the White

folk ? Or wonder why the White folkact like they want us swallowed up, but wouldn't have nobody or nothing without us?

Call us sisters,
but they Rosa Etta's wasn't raped at 11 by some white man's ghost in the family tree. Not in the same way at least.

Try to tell us we all one under the blood, but act like they ain't make us sit outside, or upstairs, or in the back to meet God on holy days.

God ain't free to the oppressed.
You gotta do some stuff.
Sit under some stuff.
Not see some stuff.

...those fans
had been donated by Black businesses, the funeral home, the cabstand. When black people paid we knew that we really wanted to see reflections of the world we lived in, not someone else's world. Even more wilder than the country churches were the tent meetings, held by the visiting evangelists from the Holy Roller churches. We thought maybe they were evangelists rather than preachers 'cause women could speak the word of [G]od at their services, could preach. In our Baptist church we had learned women were not supposed to preach, were not worthy enough to even cross the threshold of God's anointed space.

Dear God,
Why you ever fix your hands to make a Black woman? I ain't worthy of the good schools, the good water fountains, the good neighborhoods. I ain't worthy of your pulpit. You say after you looked over everything you made, it was good. Did you make Black girls? Did you make Black girl hair and Black girl lips and Black girl thighs and Black girl hips and Black girl teeth and Black girl feet and Black girl backs and Black girl necks and Black girl laughs and Black girl tears and Black girl words and Black girl ears and Black girl breasts and Black girl rest and say this was good? I feel bad. They tell me I am bad. Your people tell me to be quiet, to be covered, to be small, to make them Lord. If I'm good, then they bad. And if they good, then I'm bad. I don't think we all good cuz they seem more free in and out of your house

than me.

And I'm left wondering whose image I came from

Looking so unlike them.

Love God herself.

Looking so unlike them.

Love God herself.

Organ Plays

Now,
Before I take my seat,

And you forget this lost gospel

On purpose

Hear me when I say,

I do not wish to suggest

That the womanist lens I am proposing

Is the only way of looking at the

[World]... I do, however, propose

That this lens is true to womanist

Ideals and can, therefore,

[And can, therefore]

[And can, therefore]

Be called

Womanist.

So

Now, giving honor
Unto she who has *[kept][me] from falling,*

To the only wise God [my] Savior,
Be glory and majesty,

Dominion and power,
Both now and forever.

Amen.

Poem for Therapy Session Number 12

What if the third time
Tweet *looked over to the left*
flushed, arched and enticingly alone—
stigmata nestled between thighs and quiver—
she said to the reflecting image,
"today you will be with me in paradise?"

Tweet as God feels right—
makes me happy.
Her dark-skinned, no ass whole self
around a quarter to 3
pardoning herself
oopsing herself to shook.

And Ruth,
what if Ruth Beyoncé-*Partition*ed herself into holy—
domed her way into Jesus' genealogy?
Kneeled, perfumed and gilded,
at the feet of a rich man, ripe with liquor,
and choked until he said "marry me."

Ruth as Savior feels right—
Makes me happy.
All the self-help books on "finding your Boaz,"
missing the section on strong head game
and need.

You know how Noah sent out the raven,
and it didn't come back?
It flew in circles until the earth was dry
and then disappeared.
I sometimes think I'm the raven—
flying beaked, black and carnivorous, circling
and circling and circling until
the water unearths carcass and carrion, and then
I don't come back, and everyone
only remembers
the dove.
the dove.

Some I's are complete liars

The way the rules list steps
Like "shake well before drinking"
Or "Preheat oven before baking"
Or "See Rule 3(c) for permissible ways of identifying appellants before filing"
Or "always smile"

The fur athletic slide is the new flower top flip-flop
And trims must be had every 8-12 weeks if you want it to flow fly like the faux
you buy
Yield, Open, Stop, Slow
Thoushaltnots

There's a mouse in a sandstorm
A dead iPhone5 in a lost girl's hand
Cheap lipstick on a dead boy's body
Red carnations where pinkish white meat was
Curated for the too cool 2 to 95 year olds
Who needed a reminder that the dark is
Just a covering for the street
Thief thug thot jiving just beneath the
Surface of us all

YES BOSS
The door opens for the authorized
And the custodians only
YES BOSS
All the reading's always done
YES BOSS
Heaven's heaven even when it's a NO
And the doors have a cover charge
And the porosity of the louds is just so
As to keep the milk and honey and gold
From dropping within reach of the wrong wretched.
YES BOSS
A bowl of cherries and a slice of apple pie a with crystal
Glass of sweet tea is the gastronomic equivalent to
The American dreamfuck

YES BOSS
YES BOSS
YES BOSS
YES BOSS
YES BOSS
YES BOSS
Sure is tired BOSS

Lying in want, Wake good shepherd.
The pastures here are infamous for talking
Shit before opening to swallow us whole

I have a question: Was Lazarus wanting to come back?
Did he ask you to defy the way things were set up just to prove a point?

Could you do it again? I'm alive and asking
That you set shit up right this time,
And please don't fuck it up just to prove a point

I think most of us would rather watch the children
Imitate the wolves without hearing the guns
Imitate the stuttering Please Please Please Please
And GET DOWN GET DOWN GET DOWN GET DOWN and
Stop STOP STOP STOP STOP and *Why Why Why Why* and
OH God OH God OHHHHHH God

Oh God, I think we'd all rather like life

If the recovery weren't so

Impossible

Why The Next Poem: A Poem of Subtitles

: MY FIFTH GREAT GRANDMOTHER BORE TWO CHILDREN IN SLAVERY

: SHE DIDN'T DIE IN SLAVERY

: IN HER FREEDOM, SHE MARRIED A FREE BLACK PREACHER

: HER HUSBAND'S NAME WAS HAMILTON

: I COME FROM HER HIGH-YELLOW SLAVE SON

: HAMILTON IS A "SLAVERY AMBIGUOUS" NAME SOMETIMES

: MY GRANDMOTHER'S MOTHER USED TO SAY, WE DON'T HAVE A SLAVE NAME

: SHAME AND SEX AND SHAME AND SEX AND HOW IT MAKES PEOPLE

: SHE MARRIED A PREACHER AND MY MOTHER MARRIED A PREACHER

: MY FIANCÉ IS A PREACHER

: I AM ALWAYS THEM

: WHOSE PEOPLE ARE WE

: WHOSE WOMEN HAVE I BEEN

: I ONLY HAVE THIS TO MAKE A LIFE

If You Can't Be Free, Be A Mystery

Picture Lil' Kim dating a pastor
then unpicture everyone
making love.

What does it mean when the world breaks open
and spills yellow because you've spread your knees?

There's a televised revolution that I'm a part of,
"PrimeTime Primal,"
where Black women have sex to be like Black women
who have sex,
and the actors don't have sex in real life; So, who
are you watching really, and why
do you care, and who
isn't primitive, and aren't we
synonyms: orig·i·nal, ini·tial, ear·li·est, first,
es·sen·tial.

I apologize to monkeys
to bananas
to watermelons
to the word "plait."

I just can't wear you out
side on a t-shirt or on joggers. I can't
make a skirt out of you just because
I just can't.
That's not what my fist is holding—not what
my hips are asking for.

My mother knows this.
She chained herself to Bucknell's metal banister.
Protested for space in her school.
Held a sign with black fists breaking chains.
She doesn't use the word "nigga" now.
She just can't.

• • •

Five grandma's ago, we married a preacher
who could read and write
and give our children a name—Ham·il·ton.
A mother around 10 and around
12, then his, Ham·il·ton's, around 24
(arounding's what I have to do with us here)
(a·round·ing,
cir·cl·ing,
gain·ing world·ly ex·pe·ri·ence— be·com·ing a round thing).

Around when did she know she was naked
titties and ass? Around when did her mother know?
What did he tell her before giving her
the church and all those yellow babies?

I think next season's *Insecure* has a plot line with this.
My mother was his at 30.
Gave her bastard baby a preacher man's name too.
Gave me a clean name.
A name that didn't tell her business or mine.
A name I could wear outside.
A name it was safe to hold.

Am I a ho for hoping Rosa
orgasmed and liked staring at herself
after the bath before Sunday service
for at least a part of her life,
like Stine on *Underground*?

I don't know what my mother did before Sunday
when she was alone.

I don't know what I'll do.

● ● ●

In this episode,
we find out the saying "Hamilton is not a slave name"
is true, but Jordan and Jake wasn't really Hamiltons.
We know we Jake's kids.

We find out Rosa Etta probably started saying that to erase somethin'—
to put freedom in her sons' fists, to take the rape out of hers.

I imagine Rosa Etta liked watermelon.
My mother does.
I'm a little proud that I don't.

I imagine she loved the church house.
My mother's a deaconess.
I'm a little sad that I used to love it more,
more than I did last Wednesday.

I imagine it was hard being given a good life by a pulpit him.
The way I watched my mother do it.
Weird how now I'm doing it too.

I hope she never thought wifedom would fix her—
the way I think my mother feels it did,
the way I think it will reconcile my middle-of-the-day
wants, my morning prayer, my night-time conversation,
and how yellow makes me feel.

Currant Vigilante
In The Year of Our Lord 2017

Annette London Hester is 7.
Angelique Laila Hester is 10.

They are sisters.

They live in Garner, North Carolina.
They have 3 dogs.
They want a kitten, not a cat.
Their respective favorite colors are hot pink and eggplant purple.

On weekdays, they play outside with their brother after homework
Just because they like the air and the wide end of the block with no outlet

and running running running.

Annette London and Angelique Laila are friendly little brown Black girls.
And being friendly little brown Black girls,
they leave their brother to ask the new little brown girls if they want to play.

They think the girl wearing the pink shirt might like pink a lot.
They think the girl with the kitty cat leggings might have a kitten.
They think the girls look lonely.
They think the girls are watching them because they want to run too.
Angelique Laila runs, and Annette London scoots:

Pound Pound

KickPusssssh

Pound Pound

KickPussssssh

Pound Pound

KickPussssch

Pound Pound

Breathless,

Hi, I'm Angel and this is my sister
London. We live down there.
[points with blue chipped tip of pointer finger toward the
open].

Do you want to play with us?

I imagine the courteous, snaggletooth brown Black girl smiles.

I imagine brown Black Annette London twirling the dingy glitter streamers
on the end of her worn, pink scooter handle.

I imagine brown Black Angelique Laila firmly planted in her super-hero stance,
pretending she is Raven—dreaming up
missions for the two newest *Teen Titan* team members.

I do not have to imagine the brown girls watching them run and scoot.

I do not have to imagine the brown girls falling quiet
after receiving the invitation to run in the wide
with the two friendly, brown, Black girls.

 I do not have to imagine the one brown girl saying,

No, we don't want to play with you nigger bitches.

I do not have to imagine the second brown girl saying,

Yeah, nigger bitches.

I do not have to imagine the brown Black girls dropping their smiles and
Pound Pound KickPussssh
Pound Pound KickPussshing to their mother to say

We just asked them if they wanted to play

Angelique Laila and Annette London do not cry.
Angelique Laila and Annette London
watch their mother talk to the little brown girls' father.
Angelique Laila and Annette London don't leave the wide open anymore.

Therapy Session Number 19

My least favorite thing in the world
is drinking orange juice after brushing my teeth,
and I feel bad because I wish I didn't think of myself
first/this way—when thinking of my least favorite
thing in the world. But least favorite isn't hate—isn't
the same question.

I only drink coffee when dieting.
Something about helping my metabolism
I read somewhere it does that,
that something.

We legit go to people to hear them tell us how to be Tony the Tiger
like that's the goal. Like that's the secret we're going thirsty for.

I hate having a body.

I wish I couldn't imagine feeling my arm sawed off,
my face burned up.
Seeing other bodies that belong to me depeopled.

So much of religion is about what to do with my limbs
where to put them all.

Christ is supposed to give me salvation for my soul,
but what about my thighs, and my mouth, and my pancreas
and my mitochondria that are slowly getting tanked cuz of homemade
pesticides that farmers, I'll never meet, are killing for—
thighs and mouth still getting forced into fantastic fantasy service
all the time everywhere
no matter the height of my neckline,
that's still fighting fucking wind.

You know what thing doesn't make sense to me?
How thinking too long or too deeply on one thing
wins you a disorder
how not coming untogethered when someone or whole lots
of ones die or get killed makes you order

I can control the running;
so, I run everyday
And think about favorite colors
And try to normalize the word vagina
And the habit of blaming systems over individuals
And images of bloody panties
And the image of a twerking Phyllis Wheatley.

The Galaxy Eaters

The Galaxy Eaters count
in sevens. They shoot
helicopters down
to skip the propellers.

They dissolve watermelon *Now And Laters*
with pink tongues
while fitting footsies between whites
of clotheslines—tightrope skipping
sidestreet acts.

WUUUUUN foot
Break it down
TWOOOOO foot

They snip the tips of frozen colors
with their teeth,
spit out the transparent parts,
and suck entire glacier formations dry
just to cool off.

They trade pops of soda and waterfalls for currency,
and reek of the outside.
Bare-legged while bent over
counting bubblegum feet,
these are the playtenders.

Hands up to 85.

Punchanella in the shoe,
who do you choose?

There's a knife in your back
and the blood is coming down.

Sweet sweet baby,
I'll never let you go.

The only thing stopping these oily-elbowed,
braid-beaded, demigodic beings
are the ringers of the bells
the lights of the streets
the shouters of their names
and the beckoning of strangers.

Their kingdom falls when they
are called inside,
but maybe tomorrow,
if the pavement's just right,
maybe tomorrow
you'll get to hear them godding.

It Shouldn't Have To Be True
Because of Balaam's Donkey (Numbers 22:21-39)

I do not understand the wind in my chest—the way your control of it moves mountainous regions I miss photographing. Tell me, how did you fashion my tongue? Was there an invisible carving knife lying on my navel with instructions on how to shape my hollow—telling you to march around me until you got the sound of breaking cypress and the smell of your favorite citrus and the scratch of a coughed-up whisper?

• • •

An angel asks for your blood.
I've been telling you.
An angel asks for your blood.

Beloved, your path is a reckless one.

Tell me, how did you fashion my tongue?
Let me learn it.

• • •

In the diner, you tell me my questions about the nature of lust and the source of love and the need for love from Black women are nonsense.

In the car, you say my confusion about the body is childlike.

In the hallway, you state that I know nothing about what I'm saying about myself: How to shape my hollow.

• • •

and the scratch of a coughed-up whisper.
and the smell of your favorite citrus.
and the sound of breaking cypress
telling you to march around me until

• • •

When I was 15 and found the breath to say *You hurt my feelings when you say that,*

you said

Stop girlin'.

Was there an invisible carving knife lying on my navel
with instructions on how to shape my hollow?

• • •

Bodies of African women were translated
as a type of data
used in the freedom
of men.

African women were translated as data

Type of freedom

Bodies used

the way your control of it moves mountainous regions I miss walking

• • •

I love you
I love you
I love you
I love you
I love you
I love you
I love you

All the wind in my chest
and the cypress branch in my throat
say so.

Sequences

I heard once that 260 million years is [our] oceanic residence time.

I thought, *Damn. That means we're only, roughly, 154 years into our penance.* That means when I choked on sea water in 1996 New Jersey, I swallowed a thin shrill. I remember, it burned the thing that connects my speak

to my smell, and my ears popped. I thought, *Maybe theirs did too,* but then, I heard that our bodies were so emaciated and rawboned that we, denser than water, got guzzled—slipped right down, chasing each other without breaking to levitate. All the shark meat my auntie had me taste in Virginia,

all the bushels of Maryland Blues we laid out over newspaper on card tables, had a little bit of Zanj breast, a little Baka belly, a little Kanuri baby foot. The wide eyes of the Mbundu medicine woman, plucked apart with claws, reincarnated as the pearl Himalia Necklace at Cartier, sells for $5,750.00.

I thought, *I'll tie on my mother's pearls the next time the shore opens for me, and I'll hold my eyes open in the salt until we are in the naming ceremony, eating alligator pepper and honey and sugar and bitter kola nuts and palm oil and drinking to remind the present that water has no enemy.*

Eschatology

You're still in your body when you run
Into the burning house for help
Not crawling with the flames
You—the only upright living thing
Reach forward
Unstrange
In heat and in praise

Burnt sugar sculpture
Looking like lightning glass
Looking like magnified, melting snowflake

You are salt
And salt makes the blue yellow
And you are the sun
Turning Black

And we need less air
More flashes
More flickering

In the cellar
There's seven hundred seventy-seven bottles of wine
And the 8-year-old dachshund is tied up

Let's drink them all
And roll the dog in honey

If we make it, we will eat my foot
Feast on your right toe

But no one's coming for us

They fed the dog your daughter's tongue
Your son's feet to the cabbage heads
Your lover's elbow skin is kneaded pie crust

And we, sweetness,
Have been given the dog to tend to
And   the   vegetable   garden   to
groom And a slice of pie
And a bracelet of pearline, black-pea-like, orbs
And a Basic Instruction Before Leaving Earth
Book of law lessons they want you to lean on
As thanks for the hard part

So, we look like our mothers grabbing at what's left
With our strong stomachs and silence

So, play what we remember of them on the Victrola

Take two of these and exhale

I want to go
Naked with you

I want to go naked
With you

Can you imagine being the last one to cross the Red Sea?
A body split open for your deliverance, and you're hoping
the thought you had about slitting Pharaoh's neck
doesn't get to God's ears before you get to get out?

He's not your husband
Neither am I

And no one's coming for us

Enough looks just like this though

I swear it does
I swear

Some People Want It All

Will you eat mango meat with me

at 10:32
when I need to free something from
its skin—

when I need to suck on something sweet to
remind myself
that I don't suck at something,
when I need to flick
a switch and
be God?

You would peel,
even in fluorescent recessed lighting, the Brazil
sticker,
and we would be gods silencing
a thing—
separating a thing from the people
who planted the thing,
farmed the thing,
were culturally mandated god of the thing first,
named the thing before
I needed a guilt-free grub splayed
across white
cake plate china.

Will you run to the beauty supply with me
at 12:44
when I need to touch up on, finger through,
something virgin—when
I need to vanish something from
myself to will it to grow,
when I need to swipe plastic
and play alms reparations recipient of
wefted, bundled temple floor leftovers–
deserving?

You would ask,
even encased by faux Chanel,
ferris wheeling cubic zirconia, and
Blue Magic Just For Me,
natural brown loose body in 18
with closure? And we would be first
coming of greater gods
re-languaging a thing
re-creating in the likeness
of someone we like
re-shaping the experience of fall

            and rest

            and wrap

            and lace

—re-calling Peru and Malaysia as that time we
picked up a thing to cover my layman stabs
at hashtag natural life, and
I would swear to try again and again.

And will you rerun binge watch with me
from 7:17 until
when I need to nostalgia my body
into something like rest – when
I need to tell something to make
me cuss or cry or crack up
over opening *A Different World* or
comparing my first to Régine's last or
debating Stevie's ability to really love anybody,

and it listens?

You would *DAAAAAAAAAAAAAAAMN*
even under blankets holding half-
eaten wit and whizwit hots
and hot wings, and we
would be lesser gods of deists
watching a thing we do not touch,
hoping the thing we started
does what it's supposed to do,
like basting us in box perm and

praying through the rinse out—
a type of theocracy we'll pull out of
the Barney Bag.

Won't you
let 3:22
pass us
while we count backwards from 100
en Español resting
on capicola under towels
to keep it secret from the seagulls
because they're seagulls
by the shore
and we're bodies and bones and the
inexplicable
that keeps us
cradling Genesis
in the crick
crack open
the calabash
and make us a story
won't you
because I'm me
because you're a me
about a me
because it's about time
I get to that part in the film
that happens
between sequels
and secrets

because the difference between petty

and savage

is the *The Cask of Amantillado.*

And I think Stonehenge would have been better
with more selves than just mine only there were just me
and them who thought Britain was Britain not Britain like

Aunt Jemima was just Aunt Jemima not Aunt Jemima so
Portsmouth was watching Del Monte ships come in over
fish and chips and silence about the cost of Jamaican bananas
and loudness about war ships and waving tiny flags.

I think ballet would've been more Ailey and Jamison
if the burnt ends of my braids weren't all they asked about,
but we still drew in each other's back hair while waiting to leap
single file in pink across gray.

What I mean is
I've never told anyone about it

What I'm hearing me say is
I like beef patty and sweet tea, but

I can make you
whatever we want
when I try.

Family Picture Albums

I never fit the photos—
the narrative always seems off.
Was hash happy nigger food?
I hate it.

My grandmother eats scrapple. She says all
the pictured faces were stern and fierce,
but I'm sure the dying toddlers,

or the cold at night, or the burning piano
choked a sigh out of us.

Proverbs 31: A Kind of Pantoum for the Virtuous Woman

The universe moves in a nut sack.   Your rags for His glory.

Head, He is yours, and you are His help rib—   meaty, fallen off the bone onto the

street corner. Tender, honey-lipped, death trap, broken temple walls can be restored

in three days or the morning after.   Come get built, burdened daughter

of Sheba and Bathsheba.   God will not be pleased until you are dressed in white.

She She Shes thrashed on threshing floor for world's iniquities,   He is

your master onto the corner.   Tender honey-lipped, death trap, broken

temple walls can be restored.

Don't be lil' fast girls, holdin' hands and all hugged up.   Without Him, you

are nothing.

The universe moves in a nut sack. Your rags for His glory.

God will not be pleased until you are dressed in white   and your lips broken open
for Him.

One thing He wants.   Head, He is yours, and you, His help rib—meaty, fallen

off the bone.

She   She   Shes thrashed on threshing floor for world's iniquities,   He is your

master or your morning after.   Come get built, burdened daughter of Sheba

and Bathsheba.

Don't be lil' fast girls, holdin' hands and all hugged up. Without Him, you are
nothing.

Without His name, your lips are unclean

To the man who asked me to stop saying, "If this doesn't work"
For Jamall

Our bodies are our great grandparents' perhaps—

the of courses they would think about before transitioning to ancestral voice.

I imagine you carry weight in your face
the way she taught your grandfather to carry anger in his belly.
The way we know not to judge them for.
The way you lie on your belly at my feet and say,
We will not repeat these models.

When you say *model,*
I think of model airplanes and model cars and wonder
how something we should not touch
tells us what to want,
how to want,
dictates what to be.

I can taste our widowed granddaughter's favorite ice cream
when I suck on your left pointer finger,
and she's moving the way you taught her—
stitching herself together without long walks at midnight
reciting Poe and June and Jesus,
without forcing the grief—
like the last tray of ribs before the reunion —into the too full.

Crying between my legs, our tender-headed son asks for you.

And when he's sitting at the kitchen table,
that story summer in Chelsea—
when the heatwave wove around Pride
and the Caucasoid seminarians asked
if you were sure you lived there
and you kissed the place on his mother's chest where
her ankh scraped away the top layer of flesh—
makes the gumbo taste like a warm "thank you"
to the track star who doesn't like like him back.

I am sore between my legs from inviting you to touch me, and I regret nothing.

Annie Jane though,
her life whispers, *You are not less beautiful*
if he can't stand loving you while
the pot on the hot plate boils,

before your oatmeal is warm,
before you're kissing my neck,
before you're raising warm forkful to your lips.

Her husband was a runner,
her granddaughter's fiancé too;
so, she says *It's in your blood to dance for the damned.*

Her framed face rests on my grandmother's basement fireplace,
and I dare not run my fingers over the glass.
But I imagine my reflection in hers—
Victoria's popcorn ceiling, Victoria's
recessed lights, and my brown black
heart-shaped face over her sepia.

You lie on your belly at my feet and say, *We will not repeat these models.*

Your cinnamon words war with the salt of hers.

I leave your bed to walk the High Line and think
on a white man's words—
The boundaries which divide Life from Death are at best
shadowy and vague. Who shall say where the one ends,
and where the other begins?

Our tender-headed son asks for you.

I'm worried about the next voice.

You call me to say *come back.*

I imagine I carry fear in my throat the way the runners taught me.

The way we know not to judge them for.

We will not repeat these models.

I am wearing a yellow mini skirt, with pleats, and walking
back to your cold, rented room to cry
in your red, rented chair.

And I am moving the way our granddaughter taught me.

And you are listening.
And you say you want to drive a 1960's Mustang.
And you tell me you want to take me to China.

In 90-degree heat, we stand in line
for Morgenstern's Bourbon Vanilla,
and I believe you love me when you dance it like this.

Somewhere in the Atlantic, a lover whispers, *We will not repeat these models.*

Their lover drums it.

Your finger moves to this rhythm.
You touch me with this rhythm.
You touch me in time with this rhythm.

And we lie on our bellies with our children,
counting the seconds between lighting and thunder,
stroking their shoulders,

saying
        Open your ears,
whispering
            We have banished the spirit of fear,
singing
        You are the everything working,
working
            the way our salty bodies and cinnamon tongues have always wanted.

Rules for defining BE
In obedience to June Jordan, In rebellion against standard English

I be in my head on things sometimes. Be right in the middle of somethin', and be thrown right off by my own self on was, could, would, and maybes. I be wonderin' if I be anybody else, be anywhere else, if bein' be different. Be like, "Beyoncé don't have loans." Be like, "flies just fly." Be like, "Why I can't just be some rich man's boo?" Be foldin' clothes or be on the phone or be readin' and be like, "I can't be no balm for my block, or my hood, or this school or this world, or some man, or people I only read about." Then I be havin' to stop myself because I be forgettin' to finish what I'm doin'. Be forgettin' to be where I'm at.

It be gettin' bad tho. Walked into class and was thinkin', "Been waitin' on walkin' in here and bein' me. Been wantin' to walk down the street in Harlem and in Philly without bein' pressed up on. Be Yawnin', and they be like "Baby girl, you be needin' to be in bed earlier." Been writin' this poem and been thinkin' bout my man and been wantin' to not worry. Been wantin' to not be so hard wit him when he be wearin' his hood up. It do be cold. But he mine, and I be needin' to believe that we be alright where we be. And I be so mad that I can't be mad and I be listenin' to that Solange song, but it don't be workin sometimes. I been in my feelins on these things off and on. Be wonderin' why I gotta be so wrong and be workin' so hard to be so right and I ain't never gonna be right cuz it ain't never gonna be right. So, why I'm readin' all this Jordan and Shakespeare and Smitherman and Plath and theology and poetics and news? Why I'm doin' all this school, why I be wantin' to make more people to be where I be and they ain't gonna be able to be breathin' without grievin'? I be wantin' to put this out and be wantin' to feel right doin' it. It just ain't right or, I be somethin' I can't be right now so I can't be havin' people readin' this bein' all confused about how poetic, how genius, how well-schooled I really be. I be thinkin' too much. Was thinkin' too much. Be haffin' to say, "Girl stop. You be too much. This be what it is. This be enough."

June Jordan and her students' rules for using "To Be" (from her   essay "Nobody Mean More To Me Than You And The Future Life of Willie Jordan"(1988).

4. Use be or been only when you want to describe a chronic, ongoing state of things. He be at the office, by 9. (He is always at the office by 9.) He been with her since forever.

5. Zero copula: Always eliminate the verb to be whenever it would combine with another verb, in Standard English.

It is 2017

You have a new closeness with your grandfather
Now that he's tucked away in the military cemetery

You cannot fix your grandmother's lonely
Or your mother's tired

You try to fix yours
Plans 1-165a have failed

Suave stains the pits
Of your favorite shirt

Gorilla Snot gel flakes
Under your oily headwrap

In the heat of this NYC Poet's Dream

On the 1 Train
All of the questions start

With *where in Scripture*
Where is it written

You call the fried fish spot your church
You can't remember if you are joking

Plan 165b: don't remember, yoga,
Natural deodorant, brunch,
Harlem

Genisis, Ecdysis, Heaven

The shed browns and pinks
in the grass
on the dirt floor
the right and left hips in the mud
the back dimples
at the foot of the bed
the right breast on the chair
the left breast
somewhere
by the mailbox maybe
the mouth
in the old handbag
the hair
in chunks
in the impala's backseat
in the kitchen
on the couch cushion
with the eyes
and the fingers
fallen around
the tomato pin cushion
how
stardust fog sheds fire
double dutching
nothing to hold down during footsies
clapping numbers
the planet mars
where the babies smoke cigars
runs out of mustard
and the smile somewhere
that no one is asking for
just is

Sanctuary

The baby was resting on my left side
The woman next door said
To press until it pressed back
From the other side of the dark
Line on my belly

It moved
Only to slide out
Into the warm water
Pink
Not breathing

I dripped blood
Trails to the changing table
In the nursery
Where I would not sob
And all the women watched
And all the walls were yellow
And all the floors were gray
And I will not be naked
And I want to fuck
And a man wants to fuck me

I think Pregnancy
Is a drunk text
From God
The night before
The drunk text from the fuck
Who doesn't know

This is my eros:
the walls are never yellow
there are no mirrors
And the only stain
Is the window glass

A Theory of Light: Surviving HIM (Lifetime 2019)

Unlike sound in all its waves,
Light can travel through a vacuum—
A space devoid of matter
It can dance clean through

Stepping and tearing it up—

What a strange place to party

Step Step
Side to Side

Using our black girl feet hips and hands
To motion moves

Round and Round
Love Slide

A bouffanted Diana Ross next to HIM—
Pied Piper, Prince of the Air,
King of R&B Sound Waves

HIM—analogous to the Red-faced, sharp-featured,
"Powderpuff Girl" villain
If we don't say his name,
We can play his music

"Hey DJ! Play that Bump N' Grind"

Mix it with Smokey and some Trap Soul,
A good Chicago two step

Look at us,
Lightin' it up,
Knowing all the words

"Lil girl, watchu know bout dis?"
Step Step Side to Side
And break my heart Auntie

Patty Jackson's on the radio jockeying and cajoling
And I'm 13 at the cookout

"Now we gonna play a little game"

And I, unknowingly, hug the cousin
Who flashed my mother when she was 5

*"When I sing, I want everybody out there
To do whatever I sing, alright?"*

And everyone holds their breath
And lets me

Step Step
Clap

And I think about their golden shower jokes
And am confused

Slide

And I haven't watched the docuseries because I can't
And I know someone he asked to call him "daddy"
When he first met her,
And I somehow know there's more

Slide

What a strange place to party—
Using our black girl feet hips and
Hands to motion moves
Hot and fresh out the kitchen
Lil' mamas with bodies rollin'

Slide

"Bump Bump Bump"
Is no longer on the B2K set list,

But we still have the stills of Gayle King
And the memes.

Look at the one with 400 likes.
Gayle's the seated, unmoved Leo,
Capricorn, Aquarius, Aries, or Sag.
He's the standing, impassioned Cancer,
Scorp, Gemini, Pisces, Libra, or Virgo.

Look, do you see yourself?
Isn't it funny?

Clap in the name of love

How many licks does it take
For us to refract?

"Us" because I don't know
That he could do this to them

Slide

And all the Black preachers preached
About the sin in "Bump & Grind"

And none of them preached about the girls—
The girls who spill over the altar
Covered in prayer cloths
Seeking deliverance from
Their damnation
To being deacons' and pastors' prized playmates

Clap

"Step in the Name of Love"
Was made a Gospel song
And we brought him to church

To clap in the name of [the Lord]

Clap

Mix it with some of that new Gospel the young people like,
Add a good holy two step

Step Step
Slide

And we praised God for his deliverance
As if he were our prodigal prize

Slide

And Gayle asked him why he went to McDonald's
As if he shouldn't have or couldn't have
As if he hadn't before

As if that's the place where it all happens
As if he can't be human and harmful

Slide

And the girl didn't call him daddy—the one I know
And a lot of girls did—the ones on TV
And he told Gayle he never asks any women to call him this
And he blamed their parents
And the parents are crying
And the people are laughing
And some are still silent

And this theatre seems only to work for him and Ike

Step Step

Where   the   rape
And   the   hitting
Are still jokes

Slide

And we all still yell
At the top of our lungs
"Eat the cake Anna Mae.
Said eat the cake Anna Mae."

"We" because I don't know that he could do this to them

"We" because light can travel
through completely airless spaces

"We" because I know survivors
Because I know a friend,
I know a mother,
I know a sister
I know a cousin
I know more
Of them who travel
Through completely airless spaces

And manage to out travel the sound
Of our laughter

Are you still clapping?
I can't hear you?
Clap two times if you can hear us
Clap two times if you can finally see them

Look at all that light
Lighting

Stepping and tearing it up
Where they can out step
And out run
All the radio spin requests
All the sanctimonious Sunday sermon
Repeats all the re-grammed reposts
And the Picnic and Block Party playlists

Look at all this light
Stepping clean through all this nothing

Steppin' and tearin' it up
Without
Any sung
Direction

Never Read This Aloud. It Has No Tradition.
The Antithesis of Everything June Jordan Said a Poem Should Be

It is the dryfoot girl always lunchin'

Been that way since the devil was a boy

He stay Drawlin'

We stay Ballin'

Satan, step ya cookies up

You mad?

Cuz, Me no Conversate with the

fake's That Part

I am my favorite song

No twitter fingers necessary

This will be – is being – an everlasting love

Until it's the incoherent part and This

is the beginning

It was until that trick fixed her mouth to ask you

To prove I'm me

She got me all the way fucked up.
I   will   cut her
come up out of a bag and pop off
if tried.
my face is beat to the gods

but her body will be stomped to Hades if dat ho comes for me
Like, I would come at your neck, but

what are thoooose?
Were is the last to be verb.

Lookin' like a mufuckin uhhhhhhhhhh

This is legit the shit my mother tore out of my composition book
Right before she threw the black and white and lines across the room
Just missing my head

You could hear the pages whistle a little
When she threw it
like an axe.

He is a Black Man and the Wilderness
On Adrienne Kennedy's **Funnyhouse of a Negro**

I'm in the blackest fun house except
My favorite movie is *Funny Girl*
And my fathers' wives are Black
And I know this is not a house

My fathers are still dead
Both of them
They are both still very dead
And they are still coming for me
I am still Jesus I am
I am

Just, Patrice Lumumba is Sandra Bland
And my bald spots are clotted over
With Monistat and Jamaican Black
And there is no white face
And there is no writhing in hot bedded wetness
And my grandmother's name is Victoria
So she and Bey are the queen selves in these scenes

Rachel Dolezal is in the front row
And I scream at her braids every 18.51 seconds
Vanessa Williams yells "Cut" every 19.91 minutes
And I nae nae
And scream

Nae nae
And scream

Nae nae and scream
Until someone says
I have hanged myself

Until I have something

ENDNOTES

(In Order of Appearance)

SISTERS by GWENDOLYN BROOKS *Reprinted By Consent of Brooks Permissions.*

DEAR MOM Mommy. Since 1990. After HARMONY HOLIDAY's *Go Find Your Father (2014).*

HOS AND GRANDMAS AND AUNTIES BE LIKE Jayne Cortez & The Firespitters. "US/Nigerian Relations." *There It Is.* Bola Press, 1982.

WHEN WE PRAYED 1963—ADDIE MAE COLLINS, CAROL DENISE MCNAIR, CAROLE ROBERTSON, and CYNTHIA WESLEY murdered in The 16th St. Baptist Church bombing.

CROOKED ROOM GWENDOLYN BROOKS. "A Bronzeville Mother Loiters In Mississippi. Meanwhile, A Mississippi Mother Burns Bacon." *Selected Poems.* New York: Harper and Row, 1963. MELISSA HARRIS PERRY. *Sister Citizen: Shame, Stereotypes, and Black Women in America.* Yale University Press. 2011. "Chasity & Arianna. I Was Born By The River." Reposted by RICHBOI STREETER. YouTube. YouTube, 28 April 2015. NOTZAKE SHANGE. "dark phrases" and "graduation nite." *for colored girls who have considered suicide/ when the rainbow is enuf: a choreopoem.* New York, NY: Scribner Poetry. 1975. p.17-24. WARSAN SHIRE, "Little Wolf Little Wound." *Her Blue Body.* Flipped Eye Publishing Limited. 2015.

BLUES CLUB DANCE MUSIC MASHUP BEYONCÉ. "Why Don't You Love Me." *I Am...Sasha Fierce.* Columbia Records and Music World Entertainment, 18 Nov. 2008. NINA SIMONE. "Blackbird." *Nina Simone With Strings.* Colpix Records. 1966. BESSIE SMITH. "Need A Little Sugar In My Bowl." *Need a Little Sugar in My Bowl/Safety Mama.* Columbia Records, 1931. EARTHA KITT. *All by Myself: The Eartha Kitt Story.* Directed by CHRISTIAN BLACKWOOD. Bayerischer Rundfunk (BR). Blackwood Prods. Inc.1982. Viral Clip: "Eartha Kitt on Love and Compromise." Posted by KELLY GOURDJI. YouTube. YouTube, 20 March 2013. EARTHA KITT. "Eartha Kitt: The White House Incident." Posted by Visionary Project. YouTube. YouTube, 4 Nov. 2013. VIOLA DAVIS. "Viola Davis: 'Jim Crow did a job on us'." Posted by Women in the World. YouTube. YouTube, 12 April 2018.

17 BLACK CHURCH GIRL BLUES Cheer Squad chant, Sunday School song, and a Gospel song.

JUMP ROPE Double Dutch song. Jump rope jargon.

FRESH PRINCESS SONNETS Significant Black Americans between 1990 and 2018. Song lyrics are especially significant to Philadelphians who've enjoyed rap music between 2000 and 2018. MEEK MILL "House Party." *Dreamchasers 2.* MMG, Warner Bros. 2012.

SOME WORDS BEDEVIL, BUT MY SELF-CARE PLAYLIST LIT THO

- AUDRE LORDE. "Coal." The Collected Poems of Audre Lorde. New York, NY. W.W. Norton & Company Inc., 1997.
- CARDI B. "Bodak Yellow." Atlantic Records Corporation, 16 June 2017.
- MISSY ELLIOTT feat. LIL' KIM. "Checkin' For You." *Da Real World.* Elektra Entertainment Group Inc., 22 June 1999.
- BEYONCÉ. "Ego." *I Am…Sasha Fierce.* Columbia Records and Music World Entertainment, 18 Nov. 2008.
- MISSY ELLIOTT feat. PHARELL WILLIAMS. "WTF (Where They From)." Atlantic Recording Corporation, 22 April 2016.
- NICKI MINAJ feat. PTAF. "Boss Ass Bitch (Remix)." 2013. Web release.
- AUDRE LORDE. "A Litany For Survival." *The Black Unicorn: Poems.* New York, NY. W. W. Norton & Company, Inc. 1978.
- NICKI MINAJ. "Baddest Bitch." *Young Money Presents: Sucka Free.* Album with LIL WAYNE. Released on Spotify.com. 2010.
- TRINA. "Da Baddest Bitch." *Da Baddest Bitch.* Atlantic Records, 21 March 2000.
- TRINA (featured artist). "Make It Rain." By LIL WAYNE. *It's Weezy Baby.* The Mixtape Corner. 14 Nov. 2011.
- ALICE WALKER. Unsourced quotation.
- LIL' KIM. "Queen Bitch." *Hard Core.* Big Beat Records, 12 November 1996.
- BEYONCÉ. "Bow Down/I Been On." Released by Beyoncé on Soundcloud.com, 2013.
- TOI DERRICOTTE. "Joy Is An Act of Resistance." Joy Is an Act of Resistance." *Prairie Schooner,* vol. 82, no. 3, 2008, pp. 22–22. JSTOR.
- SALT-N-PEPA. "Big Shot." *Very Necessary.* Next Plateau Entertainment, 12 Oct. 1993.
- REMY MA. "SHEther." *Hot 97 Summer Jam.* New York, 2 June, 2017. Performance.

• RIHANNA. "Bitch Better Have My Money." Westbury Road Entertainment and Roc Nation Records. 26 March, 2015.

THEMED ZUIHITSU: MY FOURTH GREAT GRANDMOTHER AND GOD AND ME Zuihitsu: A form I learned and studied whilst under the tutelage of CHERYL BOYCE TAYLOR. Boyce Taylor defines the form with the following words:

"The Zuihitsu is a classic form from Japanese Literature that emerged sometime in the Heian Period (794-1185 AD) first seen in Sei Shonagon's *The Pillow Book*. Sei Shonagon was a court reported who documented her daily life through random thoughts, letters, poem fragments, quotes, lists of things that she liked or disliked, recipes, stories and essays among other things. She placed these notes and lists in her pillow, hence *The Pillow Book*. The word Zuihitsu means to "follow" and "brush", literally translated as "running brush." This hybrid form incorporates random thoughts, journal entries, fragments of essays, fiction, haiku, fragments of letters, fragments of poems, lines from yours and other authors, notes on pregnancy, birthing, nature, childhood, identity, family life, recipes, grocery lists, and in the last few years, emails, tweets, texts and overheard conversations.

The Zuihitsu form is rarely taught in US literature classes mainly because there is no book length study of modern Zuihitsu in Japan or the US, and because it defies definition or categorization. It is generally defined as "miscellaneous essay", in US classrooms. The Zuihitsu form was made popular in the US by Japanese-American poet Kimiko Hahn. See her Zuihitsu poems in: *The Narrow Road to the Interior*, and *Mosquito and Ant*. The Zuihitsu is generally considered poetry-prose or word collage poetry, that is made up of loosely connected fragmented essays."

MAYA ANGELOU. "Kin." *And Still I Rise*. New York, NY: Penguin Random House LLC. 1978. JUNE JORDAN. "A Poem About My Rights." *Directed By Desire: The Collected Poems of June Jordan*. Port Townsend, WA: Copper Canyon Press, 2005. bell hooks. *Bone Black: Memories of Girlhood*. New York, NY: Henry Holt and Company LLC., 1996. BEYONCÉ. "Don't Hurt Yourself." *Lemonade*. Parkwood Entertainment, 23 April 2016. RAQUEL ST. CLAIRE. *Call and Consequences: A Womanist Reading of Mark*. Minneapolis, MN.: Fortress Press, 2008. Jude 1:24-25 *KJV*

POEM FOR THERAPY SESSION NUMBER 12 Tweet feat. MISSY ELLIOTT. Oops (Oh My). *Southern Hummingbird*. The Goldmind Inc. and Elektra Records, 2002.

BEYONCÉ. "Partition." *Beyoncé.* Parkwood Entertainment and Columbia Records, 2013.

WHY THE NEXT POEM: A POEM OF SUBTITLES Familial saying/myth/desire.

IF YOU CAN'T BE FREE, BE A MYSTERY RITA DOVE. "Canary." *Grace Notes.* New York, NY: W.W. Norton & Company. 1991. MISSY ELLIOTT. "Work It." *Under Construction.* The Goldmind Inc. and Elektra Records, 2002. Familial saying/myth/desire. References to popular Black American Television shows (*Underground* and *Insecure*) and the personal branding of their actors.

CURRANT VIGILANTE Currant Vigilante" translates in Latin to "running alert" ANNETTE LONDON HESTER and ANGELIQUE LAILA HESTER (my nieces/ my love bugs).

THE GALAXY EATERS Jump rope chant from my girlhood. Hand clap and rhyme games from my girlhood (My big cousin, TANYA taught me "Knife in your back").

IT SHOULDN'T HAVE TO BE TRUE Me to my father after watching some therapists talk on television; (probably IYANLA, DR. DREW, DR. PHIL, and LAURA BURMAN). HORTENSE SPILLERS. "Shades of Intimacy: Women in the Time of Revolution." Barnard College, New York, NY. 16 Feb. 2017. Lecture.

SEQUENCES CHRISTINA SHARPE. "In The Wake: A Salon In Honor Of Christina Sharpe." Barnard College, New York, NY. 2 Feb. 2017. Panel Discussion.

SOME PEOPLE WANT IT ALL ALICIA KEYS. "If I Ain't Got You." *The Diary of Alicia Keys.* J Records, 2003.

PROVERBS 31: A KIND OF PANTOUM FOR THE VIRTUOUS WOMAN My church ladies. Proverbs 31 is a chapter often referenced as instruction for being for young girls and women in the Black Baptist tradition.

RULES FOR DEFINING BE JUNE JORDAN. "Nobody Mean More To Me Than You And The Future Life of Willie Joran." Harvard Educational Review: September 1988, Vol. 58, No. 3, pp. 363-375.

GENISIS, ECDYSIS, HEAVEN Hand clap game verse I played with friends on the playground in grade school, 1998- 2005.

A THEORY OF LIGHT: SURVIVING HIM (LIFETIME 2019) An auntie at the function or anywhere during throwbacks around young Black women.

NEVER READ THIS ALOUD. IT HAS NO TRADITION. JUNE JORDAN. "June Jordan's Guidelines for Critiquing A Poem." *June Jordan's Poetry for the People: A Revolutionary Blueprint.* New York, NY: Routledge, 1995. MARION BERNARD-AMOS (friend and former supervisor). NATALIE COLE. "This Will Be (An Everlasting Love)." *Inseparable.* Capitol Records, 1975. My Philly friends in the 99s and 2000s. ScHoolboy Q feat. KANYE WEST. "THat Part." *Blank Face* LP. 2016.

"HE IS A BLACK MAN AND THE WILDERNESS" Adrienne Kennedy. *Funny House of a Negro.* Electronic Edition by Alexander Street Press, L.L.C: 1964. 1851—SOJURNER TRUTH's "Ain't I A Woman." 1991—ANITA HILL's "Testimony to Senate Judiciary Committee.

ACKNOWLEDGMENTS

Thank you to Locked Horn Press' Read Ritual where "Rules for Defining Be" appeared in earlier form. Thank you to the Gwendolyn Brooks Estate for permitting the reprint of "Sisters" and to Dawn Okoro for allowing me the honor of using her work for the cover of this collection.

Thank you to my mother, Adrienne Jackson. Mommy you gave me pencil, paper, and Nikki Giovanni and Sonia Sanchez and Maya Angelou and James Weldon Johnson and Langston Hughes and all the Holy Ghost Baptist Black interpretation of Scripture. For my sensitivity, my art form, my sisters, my slick mouth, and for always believing I was worth it, I thank you. Thank you to my grandmother Victoria B. Tolbert who framed the first poem I wrote when I was 12 and shared it with everyone who entered her home. Thank you to my aunt, Annamarie Bell. Every day I miss you, every day I hear you. To Annie Jane, Lilly Blue, to Chaine Hamilton, to Rosa Etta, and to all the women I come from: I honor you, I thank you, I be you.

Thank you to my teachers and mentors: Farah Jasmine Griffin, Lynn Melnick, Alan Gilbert, Joshua Bennett, Cheryl Boyce Taylor, Kamilah Aisha Moon, Elizabeth Alexander, Rickey Laurentiis, Monica Youn, Deborah Paredez, Dorothea Lasky, Alice Quinn, Lucie Brock Broido, Richard Howard, Salamisha Tillet, Yolanda Wisher, Peggy Robles-Alvarado, Jean Corey, Helen Walker, Tricia Johnson-Collins, Maude Atwell, and Dr. James Cone.

Thank you to the spaces that incubated me during the process of writing this work: KP and Philadelphia's Pecola Breedlove and the Freedom Party, Philadelphia's Modern Lit Workshop, The Public Libraries of Philadelphia and New York City, The Schomburg Center for Research in Black Culture, Cave Canem's "Bush Medicine" workshop space, Columbia University's Institute for Research in African American Studies, The Bookloft of Great Barrington Mass., Poetry Society of America, Lincoln University of Pennsylvania, Columbia University, University of San Diego, and every Black church where the folk were warm, the tea sweet, the pantyhose opaque, the service long, and the chicken fried to perfection.

To my Columbia writers workshop friends who read over and helped to organize the pieces in this manuscript—Carly Inghram, Rob Crawford, Rodney Leonard, and Sarahann Margaret Swain—thank you. A special thank you to Coco Wilder who also carefully read over the poems in this manuscript, and to Cyree Jarelle Johnson and Chelsea Sylviolet Smith whose reading of my work made me feel less alone when it mattered most. To my husband, my partner, my love, Rev. Jamall Andrew Calloway, PhD, thank you for supporting me and for believing in my work, even when I struggled. You mine and I'm blessed to share you with you.

Many thanks to Erica Hunt for reading the work and deeming it necessary and urgent. And to the Kore Press Institute team, thank you for your continued long-suffering commitment to your mission.

A special thanks to Dr. Latinia Shell, Marion Bernard-Amos, and Vanessa Gang for showing me I was ready to write again. To Sheba Ebhote and Ashley Regis who let me sleep on your futon when I was taking that long drive from Philly to NYC, I am eternally grateful. Thank you to Briannah LaMarr, Ishea M. Jennings, Joy M. Christian, Olufemi Adedoyin, Amber Sanders, Charlotte Cirino, Ronisha De Luzio, Ashley Hester, Aigner Jackson, and Anitra Jackson for being my squad, my prayer partners, my sage burners, the ones to speak my own name over me and twerk with me upon my prodigal return home to myself. I love you all more than I will ever be able to express. To my family, my mothers, my fathers, my grandfathers, my siblings, my nieces, my nephews, my aunts, my uncles, my godparents, and host of cousins, both play and blood, thank you for saving me a plate, for braiding my hair, for giving me my many names, and for being my home.

To 4C Jesus, Oya, and Rosa Etta, thank you for sustaining me.

Lastly, Asé to every Black Woman Poet and every Black American Woman Poet and Story Teller who writes and has written and will write because what else is there but being a "difficult miracle." My words live in your hands. I study among you. I am you.

ALEXIS V. JACKSON is a Philadelphia-born, San Diego-based writer and teacher whose work has appeared in *Jubilat, The Amistad, La Libreta, Solstice Literary Magazine,* and *805 Lit* among others. Jackson earned her MFA from Columbia University's School of the Arts and her Bachelor of Arts degree in English from Messiah University. Erica Hunt selected Jackson's forthcoming debut collection, *My Sisters' Country* (Fall 2021), as second-place winner of Kore Press Institute's 2019 Poetry Prize. She has served as a reader for several publications, including *Callaloo* and *Bomb Magazine.* Jackson lectures in the University of San Diego's English Department. She has also taught poetry at her alma mater, Messiah University.

COLOPHON

My Sisters' Country comes to you, dear reader, by the dedicated in-house and out-of-house team at Kore Press Institute. KPI is currently housed in Room 201 of the Dunbar Pavilion—an African American Arts and Culture Center named after the poet Paul Laurence Dunbar, and Tucson's first and only segregated school for African-Americans up until 1952. We acknowledge where we live and work is on occupied Tohono O'odham and Yaqui ancestral lands.

My Sisters' Country is the Second Place winner of the 2020 Kore Press Institute Poetry Prize, chosen by poet and esteemed judge, Erica Hunt. This poetry collection was short-listed by our team of readers, poets Marilyn McCabe, Gail DiMaggio, Kyle Laws, Vidhu Aggarwal and Ann Dernier. Our industrious staff included Lisa Bowden, Ann Dernier, Tina Howard, Casely Coan, Rosalie Morales Kearns, Rylee Carrillo-Waggoner, and our Fellowship recipients: Abby Johnson, Annamae Sax, Aisha Al-Amin, Ari Schill, and Michelle Lee Salnaitis. Gratitude to our book designer, Sally Geier, and to you, our readers for keeping the candle burning.

We wish to acknowledge all our family members who made room for our work at home, at the kitchen table, with the light on all night, with internet interruptions, with power outages and fires raging, with smoke filled skies, supply scarcities, soaring infection rates, and unbearable losses. And also during that long period of "delivery or drive-through" for everything including vaccinations. We hold you closer than ever, with deep gratitude for your expansive hearts, especially in confined spaces.

KORE (kor-ay) is Greek for daughter and another name for the mythic Persephone—the goddess taken into the underworld who wrestled with darkness (and its enticements, sexiness and fraught, lonely trade-offs). She reemerged periodically above ground only after her mother and Hades struck a deal over how to share their beloved. Kore's appearance above ground inspired the change in season: from winter to spring, fallow to fruit, dark to light, struggle to innovation. The Kore/Persephone myth has taken on intense meaning during this time of global pandemic where we wait in fallow, in an "underworld life," for a little more light to come lead us to a new place.

At the time of publication, we are all living this more intensely than ever. Our goal the last twenty-eight years at Kore Press Institute has been to collectively effort toward building more just and radically connected communities with creative, innovative, and intersectional works that amplify and celebrate all women's voices, especially the most marginalized. You can support one of the country's oldest feminist, literary publishers by buying books directly from Kore or at an indie bookseller near you. Become a sustaining member of the Press and learn about KPI's award-winning programs by visiting korepress.org.